BEHIND THE MASK

Laurie Forrest

 FriesenPress

One Printers Way
Altona, MB R0G 0B0
Canada

www.friesenpress.com

Copyright © 2024 by Laurie Forrest
First Edition — 2024

ISBN
978-1-03-918113-7 (Hardcover)
978-1-03-918112-0 (Paperback)
978-1-03-918114-4 (eBook)

1. BIOGRAPHY & AUTOBIOGRAPHY, PERSONAL MEMOIRS

Distributed to the trade by The Ingram Book Company

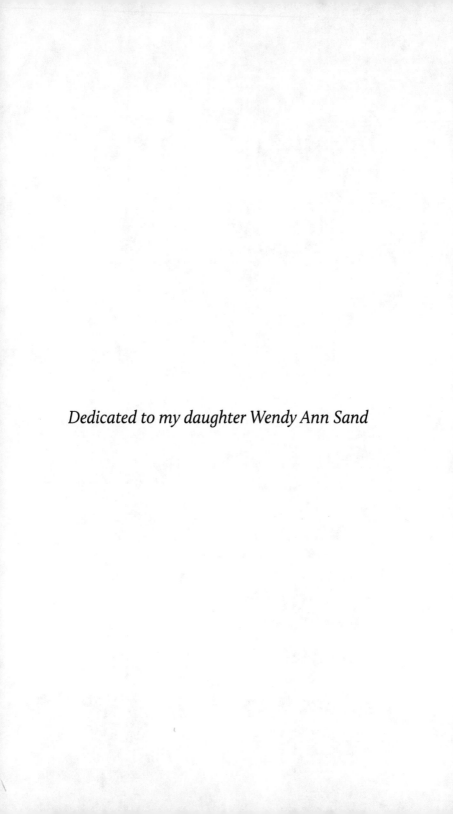

Dedicated to my daughter Wendy Ann Sand

Table of Contents

A Black-and-White Photo. 1

My Dad. 5

Quiet. 11

Lost 14

The Ocean 18

Were We Poor? 22

A Trip to Winnipeg 26

Mean Girls 30

The Palace 34

Broken 38

A Life-Changing Moment. 42

A Hot Wind 44

Tears 47

Running for My Life. 52

Fragile. 58

The Visit. 62

Fire 67

Michael. 72

Ferris Wheel 75

Katherine 79

Syd. 82

Annie. 85

Homelessness 91

Women's March 94

Life Behind the Mask. 97

Goodbye, My Friend 100

Wrapping Up. 105

A BLACK-AND-WHITE PHOTO

She stared at me from her passport photo, a sad and depressed expression on her beautiful young face. Her eyes were hauntingly expressive—a rich deep brown as I knew them to be, but in this picture, they looked dark and penetrating and, while alluring, they had a blank nothingness about them. Her lovely full lips were a bit downturned, and she looked as if she were about to cry.

This picture haunted me as I viewed it repeatedly. It was my mom as she was about to depart from her home in Northern Ireland for a land unknown to her . . . Canada . . . and with a man who was now her husband whom she hardly knew. She was pregnant with me.

Sitting with her as a five-year-old, I traveled through the dark brown leather photo album containing her old black-and-white photos. It was heavy for me to carry but I would bring it to my mom so we could go through it together. She enjoyed reminiscing while viewing these pictures with me.

"Those were such happy days," she commented.

In the photographs, I remember so clearly, she is at the beach . . . probably Port Rush, just outside of Belfast, bundled up in a long coat and scarf. My mom is a tiny thing—only 4 '11" and all of ninety-five pounds. She sits across the laps of some young men in uniform with their bomber jackets zipped up against the cold. Her dark, wavy hair is lifted by the wind as she throws back her head in obvious delight, a look I had rarely seen on her face.

"I have such fond memories of those war days!" my mother said on many an occasion.

In retrospect, this seems so ironic to me as they were terrible days to be alive with all the ugliness of that war. But it was the era of her youth. It was her coming of age, her music, her fashion, and it was also a time of terror and death. I often wonder if the heightened panic, fear of dying, the overall excitement of war and all that it brought to her life was a high that she would never get back again. Each morning must have brought accelerated delight at just waking up, especially after a night of being relentlessly bombed by the Germans.

Whenever we come to her passport picture, I ask, "Why are you so sad in this, Mommy?"

She answers, "I was unhappy because I was leaving home and did not know if I would ever see my family again. And maybe I was feeling a bit sick because I was just pregnant with you."

Somehow, I connected her leaving home and being pregnant with me as the reason for her sorrow. I was so young yet felt such discomfort in her pain as it was reflected to me so clearly in this picture.

My mom was depressed a lot of the time. I saw that ghostly look on her face often in real life and it hurt me. Did I feel responsible for her grief, or did I just love her and want her to be happy—especially now that I was in her life?

Later as an adult, I was to find out what led up to her forlorn expression. Why did she marry my father, a man she did not love? A man who asked her to marry him after a Red Cross dance because he was smitten and dazzled by her. A man she turned down because he was not a Catholic—a more benign excuse. A man who later converted for her and sent her word that he was now a Catholic and they could marry.

And a church that called the shots for her.

"He was becoming a Catholic for me, what else could I do?" was the answer she gave me.

In that revelation, she freed me from the notion

that I might be culpable for her depression. I also understood the anger she felt for my dad for loving her and converting for her and for the way this caused her own inner anger to turn onto him. It is a consolation to me that I questioned and chose my conscience over Catholic Church teachings. Sure, I made mistakes, but only I was responsible for them.

Mom had made some poor decisions for many wrong reasons, and on some level, she knew this as the camera clicked. This black-and-white photo captured the future of unhappiness that she envisioned for herself.

MY DAD

"*Tell us about the war, Daddy!*"
      He would shake his head and say, "*The war is something that you do not want to hear about as it was a painful time.*"
"*Did you kill people?*"
No response! Once he did share with me that on returning from a mission he was informed as to what planes did not make it back. He lost dear friends. His heart was broken over and over. He became totally despondent, and as new recruits came into his barracks, he would not introduce himself or want to know who they were. He could not take any more heartache. There was that distant, pained look in those gray-green eyes of his that were shadowed by the scar when he spoke of this.

My dad's name was Harry. When he was nineteen years old, he joined the Royal Canadian Air Force and was shipped off to Belfast, Northern Ireland, to fight against Germany. All the men in the air force were trained to be pilots and the best were the ones who flew the airplanes. The others took different positions within the plane. My dad was a bomber pilot. The war for him started in 1939, when he began his missions. His squadron was to protect the submarines and the battleships. Unlike Americans who were released from combat after a certain number of missions, should they survive, those RCAF pilots had to continue flying until the war was over—or they were, whichever came first.

My dad had a long, dark scar on his face that began just above his right eye and inched all the way down his face into his cheek. As my little girl finger traced that scar down his sweet face as he held me in his lap, I asked what happened.

"I survived an airplane crash," he told me.

His aircraft was headed back to Belfast after completing a mission protecting a few battleships crossing the Atlantic for Europe. The men were tired, and some were playing card games. My dad was playing a hand, but another pilot wanted into the diversion, so, my dad gave up his place. He then curled up in the tail part of the plane and fell asleep.

He woke up outside the plane, bleeding from his head and face, having trouble staying conscious. Nine of his friends were dead, a fact I found out from reading his flight journal after his death. The plane was in splinters. He started to wander and was finally picked up. He was able to show the rescue team where the seven others were who were also severely injured. It turned out it was quite overcast and foggy that night while they flew back from their mission, and the visibility was bad. The engineer had not brought them high enough to miss the top of Knocklayd Mountain in Northern Ireland.

My father was hospitalized and patched up. Once mended, he was sent back to fly until the war ended in 1945.

My dad was one of the gentlest men I have known. He was soft-spoken and kind, with an immeasurable amount of patience, and nothing seemed to ruffle his feathers. He was so good about playing with us children and giving us love and attention after work, even though he must have been so tired. Being with us brought him pleasure, I could tell. He had that Canadian dry sense of humor that he enjoyed teasing us with.

As I grew up and started to learn more about WWII, I was rather surprised that my father was even able to participate in something so horrible as this war and come home the warmhearted and tender man that he was. An experience like that at such a young age could really mess you up! He seemed unfazed by it except for the sadness that would show itself at times. However, the reality of this understanding for him was that when a crisis happened in our family—the split open heads, ear infections, broken cars, heart murmurs, and other family traumas that occurred over the years due to having six children—it was nothing to him compared to what he knew as a young man in battle. He had learned to appreciate the "usual" life and to experience that normality in stride—and with a calm that always made me feel safe.

Flying during the fifties and sixties was not widespread . . . at least not for our family, as it was costly.

My dad did not want to fly ever again after the war. He drove everywhere, including cross-country trips to Winnipeg, Canada, in our broken-down car. Winnipeg is just above North Dakota, and we were living in Los Angeles, California. These trips were quite miserable for all of us. However, in 1978, he got word that his mother was dying and he needed to get to Canada quickly.

He asked me if my daughter, Wendy, would fly with him to Canada. It was summertime, so Wendy was not in school. She was ten years old, loved to fly, and was crazy about her grandpa. Being one of six children and never having alone time with Dad, I was a bit envious of my little girl but also excited for her.

Dad told me: *"I want your grandma to meet her great-granddaughter."*

On some level though, I knew that he wanted the company. He could not be afraid if Wendy was with him.

As he aged, he started to become forgetful and, eventually, around the age of seventy, had the beginnings of dementia. I had read some articles about the testing of World War II pilots with bad head injuries. The studies showed that many of them went into early Alzheimer's. It was a frightening time for Dad. It was my first time seeing him anxious and upset. The upside was that now he wanted to talk about the war days. He remembered all his buddies and the fun times they'd had just before they went off on a mission.

He started to repeat the same stories over and over. I could tell he still missed them.

In his last days, he again showed me his loving courage in approaching the end of his life.

"Laurie, I am a blessed man," he said to me. *"I received fifty-eight more years of life, which was more than most of my buddies. I was able to be married, and know the joys of having you children, and seeing my grandchildren."*

He said this to me again just two days before he died, and on that day, as I held his hand and felt the warmth leave his body, I sensed his spirit there in the room, and I knew that he was happy to be on his way to meet those long-lost buddies once again.

QUIET

Quiet as a mouse. That was me. Being silent worked at home and in school. The definition of conduct for our grammar school was to be still and not unruly. This was not only important to Mom and Dad but to my teachers, and I never failed in that area. I didn't even have to try as I liked being quiet and received an A every year.

There is a downside. Our culture promotes speaking out—as in "The squeaky wheel gets the oil." So, I tended to not get what I wanted. Learning comes about by asking questions—of which I had lots, but I was afraid to raise my hand and ask them for fear of getting ridiculed or the teacher getting upset at me for not paying attention.

You see, I was a bit of a daydreamer, and my mind would wander off into my imagination. This fancy of mine was not appreciated until one year in grammar school.

My third-grade teacher encouraged me to use my

creative mind:

"Your pensiveness is a lovely quality, Laurie," she would tell me. "You want to utilize it. Write down those thoughts and dreams."

Even in her habit, Sr. Mary Trinita was beautiful! I would guess now that our class was her first experience in teaching. She was young, patient, and kind, relating well to eight- and nine-year-olds. Her perfectly aligned features, porcelain skin, and soft, shimmering blue eyes made her so pleasant to look at, even as covered up as she was. And that joyous smile of hers was so contagious . . . a reward.

My father noticed her loveliness too and would look for any reason to visit my class, one excuse being to bring in a forgotten lunch—or did he hide it?!

He would share with me later: "She is not only a good woman but gorgeous to boot."

"Dad, you come to class just to look at her!"

"You might be right on that one," he would respond.

It was fun to see those two flirting together, although I didn't realize this at the time. Looking back, I realize that he was probably only thirty-three years old—a young man indeed caught under her glorious enchantment—and she, a youthful woman, obviously enjoyed the attention of my dad.

Much later, once the nuns had lost their habits, I heard that she had pretty red hair . . . long and wavy. Once Dad had mentioned to me that he thought she might be a redhead. At the time I wondered why he would say that as that head gear of her habit never let a strand of hair peek through. What did I know? Dad knew she could only have red hair with that lovely complexion.

This nun passed on her love of reading by showing us how to drop into new lands and adventures through books. Reading was assigned to us as homework, and we spent a good portion of our school day reciting. The class was broken into groups: monkeys, giraffes, and lions. Lions, which I was a part of, were the top group, and we would be asked to read out loud. When she called on me, I would stand and read for her alone. No one else existed and I read with animation and expression, wanting to impress her.

She would excitedly clap for me. To have this woman, whom I adored, appreciate and applaud me sent me reeling with delight.

She saw me as no other teacher had before.

A quiet person can be somewhat invisible and mysterious and Sr. Mary Trinita taught me to honor that part of myself.

LOST

"Where did the house go?"
I had been playing and exploring in the backyard of my folks' friends. They lived in the San Fernando Valley, and their home was set among the many orange groves. They were the couple that sponsored my family to come to the United States. There was no fence and I had wandered off without paying attention. I looked around to go back into the house and it was not there!

"Oh no! What if I can't find it!"

I was five years old and very frightened. I started to cry. I wandered down one street and then another looking desperately for the house. Finally, I came to a busy street, with lots of cars and intersection lights. I walked to this street. Looking back, I wonder now if it was Ventura Boulevard.

I was still crying when a woman approached me and said, "Little girl, are you lost?"

I nodded. She took my hand and walked me to a phone booth. We stepped inside and she made a phone call. Once we left the box with the phone, we waited for I don't know what. Along came a police car, which slowed and stopped in front of us. I wonder now whether the woman got in with me or if I was placed in the back seat by myself. I do remember that I was no longer scared, though I am not sure why I wouldn't be. The policemen or the woman who found me must have convinced me that they would get me home somehow.

Once in the police station, I was in my glory. I don't think I had ever experienced so much positive attention and fun. I had several men talking to me, playing with me, and buying me ice cream.

Time just sort of stood still for me.

Then my dad and his friend walked through the door. The look on his face brought me back to reality as he looked like he had just seen a ghost. It was white and drawn with both relief and fury. I went from extreme happiness to a feeling that I had done something terribly wrong. I was little and didn't know what my dad had to do in order to leave the police station with me.

I do recall that once my mom, dad, and two little sisters were on our way back to our house in Mar Vista, my dad told me that I had terrified my mom and everyone and that this was not a good thing. I felt that I would be punished once we got home.

I was the one who was lost. What about me? I thought. *I was terrified too.*

I worried and wondered with those mixed emotions of a child. In dread, I got ready for bed while Mom and Dad put Maureen, the baby, back to sleep. I jumped into bed troubled about what would come next.

Both my mom and dad came to tuck me in. They told me that they loved me so much and that when they could not find me, they became scared as to what might have become of me. They spent many hours feeling this way while looking for me. Finally, they called the police and found me. When my dad saw how happy I was after what they had all been through, he became furious with me. Of course, I was told never to do that again. And, believe me, I pretty much stuck close to home after that incident.

Direction has always been a challenge for me. I sometimes picture myself on the little girl assembly line about to be born and the part of my brain that determines direction being mistakenly left out.

Today, I understand those mixed emotions of the parent, having lost my own little girl at Venice Beach one day when she was two.

Wendy and I were sharing a blanket. She was

digging in the hot sand and carefully filling her sand pail. I took this opportunity to quickly read a bit of my book. Once I looked up, she was no longer there! I frantically and briefly looked around and then dashed toward the water. Oh my God, where was that little munchkin of mine? At the water's edge, I ran up one end of the beach and down the other end to the lifeguard station and explained to the young man there that I had lost my little girl. He asked me to describe her, and I did, experiencing the excruciating pain of worry and the gnawing bile creeping from my stomach and burning into my mouth. It was one of the longest and most painful ten minutes I'd ever experienced. Then I had the wonderful excitement of finding her but wanting to just shake her for wandering off like that.

It was a déjà vu moment, and I then understood both sides of being lost.

THE OCEAN

The young lifeguard plucked me out of the water after I had tumbled in and out of the waves over and over as if in a washing machine. We were at Venice Beach and there was a strong undercurrent that sucked me into the sea, and I was breathing in saltwater. After the first gulp, which hurt dreadfully, I felt nothing but a floating sensation as round and round I went while my short seven years of life flashed before me. I envisioned, in my mind's eye, Mom and Dad crying at the loss of me, which made me sad, but since I was preparing for my First Communion, I believed I was going to God, so was not afraid.

Once in the lifeguard's arms as he reached the hard sand and was carrying me out of the surf, I began choking something fierce, trying to get rid of the water in my lungs. The lifeguard then handed me over to my dad and I threw my arms around his neck and clung for dear life, and the sweet safety I felt in that moment.

But before this, Mom was getting a reprieve from mothering while my dad took the three of us girls down to the edge of the ocean to frolic in the waves. Neither I nor my younger sisters knew how to swim, so we just lay in the wet sand and let the trickle of frothy waves roll over us. While there on my stomach moving my arms above my head, pretending to swim, I felt a pulling sensation and I gripped the wet sand with my little fingers only to continue moving out into the water. Daddy was yakking with someone he knew and wasn't really paying attention. Being extremely frightened, I weakly called out: *"Dad??"* By this time though, I was being gobbled up by the waves.

Once safe in my dad's arms, we joined Mom up on the sand where we had parked our beach gear. She tells me: *"Ah . . . here I was enjoying the sun, just relaxing on the sand, not having to worry about you girls. I was having so much fun observing two young women flirting with the extremely handsome lifeguard when he jumped up, threw off his hat, and took a leap off the lifeguard station heading toward the water."*

My mom then raced down to see who was drowning only to get sick to her stomach as she saw a little chartreuse bathing cap bobbing far out into the water and knew it was me, as both the lifeguard and Dad swam desperately to catch up.

This was not the last "almost drowning" experience I had while at the beach. Even only knowing how to 'dogpaddle' by then, I would body surf with my high school friends at Santa Monica beach. After getting pummeled by massive waves at age sixteen in Malibu and eventually being pulled out of the ocean by my friend, did it finally hit me to stop tempting the ocean. It was then that my fear of the ocean took hold of me.

From then on, nightmares about tidal waves have plagued me. In the dream, it is always a dark, ominous day with enormous waves that build up to the size of skyscrapers and are ready to pounce and swallow me up. I wake as they are just about to break.

I was twenty-six by the time I did learn to swim. While in the stands at the YMCA in West Los Angeles watching Wendy, my daughter, taking her swim lessons, I signed up for the evening adult swim classes. I can now float, and do the breast and back stroke as well as freestyle. Though not a strong swimmer, I can hold my own in pools and lakes, but the ocean still has power over me as it is a mighty force to be reckoned with and I have great respect for it.

I take my granddaughters to the beach when

they come to visit. They are good little swimmers and are cautious when skipping in and out of the waves. Since I continued to be aware of the water's strength, we sat right in front of the lifeguard station, and I did not take my eyes off them for even a minute.

WERE WE POOR?

T he late fifties and sixties were hard times for my folks as my mom became pregnant three more times and it seemed that Dad was on strike a lot working for the RTD as a bus driver. There was always food on the table and a roof over our heads when living in Venice. However, having enough money always seemed a struggle. I never considered myself poor in those days. I just assumed everyone in our neighborhood was in the same boat.

We lived next door to another young family with two children our age. Phillip, the dad, drove a Helm's Bakery truck. When he finished his route, he would get to keep the bread that didn't sell, and he would share the day-old bread with our family.

Bill Lennon, the father of the not-yet famous Lennon Sisters, was a milk man who worked for Alta Dena and delivered two bottles of milk to us each Monday. Those bottles would have to last the whole week, so my mom would divide the milk evenly among the six of us. Mom and Dad made sure we got the milk. They did splurge on butter for themselves, which they used sparingly, and we got the margarine, which we loved.

My sisters and I would each get a quarter to go to the movies at Fox Venice Theater on Lincoln Blvd. My mom needed a break from our relentless fighting, and we could be totally engrossed watching two double features with a cartoon in the middle. In the summertime during the intermission, the theater would provide talent shows. One year I developed enough courage to get on stage and sing. The song "Que Sera Sera," sung by Doris Day, was a favorite of mine, so I chose that as my show-tune. I WON! The prize was a board game whose name I've forgotten.

One year, at Christmastime, Dad was on strike so we could not afford a Christmas tree. The three of us girls were so disappointed and sad but understood the financial difficulty my folks were experiencing, which I find somewhat amazing at our young ages. Mom told us that it would be a difficult year for Santa, which I found puzzling as how did she know this about Santa Claus, who lived in the North Pole. Our mom was so adamant about this that I did not expect to get the "Kathy Doll" I had asked for.

Christmas Eve arrived, and it was late at night . . . well, around 8 p.m., our bedtime. We were listening to a story on the radio together—probably "The Shadow"—as we still did not have a TV set. A knock came to our door. It was our neighbor Phillip and in his hand was a Christmas tree! He said:

"When finishing up my bread deliveries, and returning home via Venice Boulevard, I noticed that the tree lot on Venice and Grandview were selling their Christmas trees for a dollar, so I picked one up for you!"

Dad went out to the garage to bring in the ornaments. Mom made hot cocoa and we all decorated the tree that night. The next morning, lo and behold, my "Kathy Doll" was under the tree, as well as many other presents. The stockings were loaded with oranges, nuts, and Life Savers! It seemed like a miracle to me! I was so very happy!

A few years later when I was nine, we finally had a TV set, the last family on the block to get one, and while watching *Miracle on Thirty-Fourth Street* with a young Natalie Wood, I learned there was no Santa. There is a part in the movie where Natalie says: *"Santa Claus is not real!"*

Gerry, Maureen, and I were sitting cross-legged right in front of the screen while Mom and Dad were on the couch against the wall behind us and

Mom was knitting away. I looked back and said: *"But there is a Santa, right?"*

Mom shook her head from side to side. I was devastated as my bubble burst. I jumped up and moved onto the sofa and cuddled up to both and cried.

After I got over this traumatic bit of knowledge, I started to understand clearly all that went before: Mom's warning that Christmas would be limited, and yet I had never been disappointed. How did they do this? The money used to get us what we asked for was almost more of a wonder then the Santa story. I looked at my folks in awe.

Years later with three more little ones added to our family, I found out that Mom would open a Christmas bank account and pay into it every month. When shopping at Sears throughout the year, she would put toys and clothes on layaway for the holiday, and then pay for it all the week of Christmas with the bank money.

What fun it now was to keep the Santa story alive for my younger brothers and sister. My parents created a holiday full of richness and joy every year that I will never forget.

We did have wonderful times together regardless of the lack of money. We were rich indeed!

A Trip to Winnipeg

Remember the slogan "It's the journey, not the destination, that matters most"? My family provided a more humbling experience in 1960. Eight of us were crammed into my father's ten-year-old clunker of a station wagon—Mom, Dad, three teens, and three tots, two still in diapers—departing Los Angeles for Winnipeg, Canada:

Eight of us!

In the middle of August!

In a car with no air conditioning!

Two stalwart parents and six sweaty, cranky, restless kids, unable to move for hours at a time on this trip from you know where. The little ones behaved better than the three of us teenagers, who were miserable and fighting with each other in the back seat.

I was almost fifteen, and not happy about taking this family trip to Winnipeg. Ah . . . to have been able to stay home in Venice with my high school friends at Santa Monica Beach not harnessed to the family would have been my idea of heaven. But no choice was offered to me.

It was a misadventure I had put behind me until my sister-in-law, Terri, transferred pictures from my mother's photo album onto a DVD and there we were in living black and white.

Mom hated these trips. She didn't like Dad's family. Now here she was on a 2,000-plus mile torture trip with two kids still in diapers in a car that might break down at any moment. I smile when I look at that DVD photo of my mom, knowing what was behind her smile: *Somebody get me out of here!* Dad tried to keep the peace in his usual laid-back way, turning around, warning us over and over:

"Girls, please keep quiet back there! Stop that bickering!"

He was hot, flustered, and pissed, and the look on his face said it all. As we shut up, Mom would start in:

"Why do we have to make this journey for your family?"

"What have they ever done for us! They don't even like me!"

"Why can't we get a decent car?"

You get the picture. None of us made it easy on my father.

Mom had packed lunches of sugar sandwiches, consisting of margarine-coated white bread and sugar. We would stop for dinner at a diner in whatever small town we landed for the night. Our family budget restricted us from ordering what we wanted, and our parents picked out our meals for us.

I don't recall how much of the grandeur of the southwest we enjoyed during that jaunt. Did just trying to survive the blazing hot conditions in our beat-up brown and yellow station wagon blind us from noticing the reds, oranges, and pinks resplendent in the painted desert of Arizona and New Mexico? The heat seemed never-ending, from the desert and then heading north through Oklahoma, Kansas, and Nebraska, squished together, hot air pouring in on us from the furnace outside until we reached the next level of "Dante's Inferno," humidity adding to our misery as we made our way through each succeeding state and into the Dakotas.

Mom didn't have the elbow room in the front seat needed to change Mark and Eileen's diapers—cloth ones in that pre-Pampers era—so the already unbearable air became infused with the powerful stench of urine and ammonia, which we all hoped might kill the bugs hopping a ride with us. The enormous flying beetles, probably an inch long with jet-black rigid shells, made a beeline inside our car, landing on the babies' pee-soaked bottoms. Terrified, we yelled and swatted, hoping to force these creepy critters out.

Dad was done with the chaos and stopped in one of those sleepy towns in South Dakota to look for a motel. Finally! An oasis! A small motel with a pool! We got two rooms for the eight of us. However, there was still no air conditioning, and the debilitating heat didn't seem to bother the fleet of flying beetles lining the walls like planes on a runway, ready to attack. In the swimming pool, we drowned our sorrows for hours, until we were completely waterlogged and so wiped out that even the bugs couldn't bug us.

We were near the end of our journey; in another day we would arrive at my grandparents' home, and conditions did improve a bit as they had screened-in porches to shut out the bugs, but not the heat. As we visited with family, my sisters and I had time to frolic around out of doors with our cousins. But this didn't stop the tune "California here I come" from playing in my head for the rest of that week or the trip home.

I have never returned to Winnipeg . . . not even by plane.

Mean Girls

"*L*et's ditch her!*"

I heard one of the girls say. Hurtful words to an anxious fourteen-year-old who had just entered a new school. Words that still sting today.

"Let's take the first bus. It'll fill up and there will not be any room for her."

They took off, the four of them, into the crowd of high school kids about to take the long ride home after an away football game. The pain of this rejection scratched my heart with an unexpected sharpness and the tears came uninvited as I made my way to the third and last bus.

The first one on, I walked all the way to the back and sat by the window on the wall-to-wall seat, hoping I would go unnoticed. By then I was sobbing. What was wrong with me? Why didn't they like me?

The bus started to fill up. I tried desperately to stop crying, looking out the window at nothing, pretending I was lost in thought. I just wanted to be left alone.

It was turning out to be the sophomore year from hell. This was unlike Bishop Conaty High School in Los Angeles, where I spent my freshman year. And here, despite being the rare white face in a sea of black and brown, I was accepted and embraced for the insecure, small, bashful white girl I was. What a juxtaposition compared to the reception I received at this school in Santa Monica. Since I did know one girl from grammar school, I clung to her, even though her other friends treated me like a pariah from the moment we met. They routinely spoke down to me or excluded me from their conversations or just left me alone in the schoolyard.

How unsure I was at age fourteen, a difficult time under the best of circumstances. I wasn't very cool. I looked like a little girl and was acutely quiet. I had hairy legs and begged my mom to let me shave them, but she wouldn't budge. It just wasn't done in her home country of Ireland and that, she informed me, was that! Of course, the Mean Girls pounced on it and called me "chicken legs." They were relentless.

Finally, the hurt cut so deep, I risked my mother's wrath, saved my allowance, and returned from the local Thrifty's with a box of Nair, a chemical hair remover. I emerged from my nightly bath with the unsightly hair gone. The next morning, I dreaded what I was about to tell Mom.

"Oh, no!" she shrieked. "Tell me you didn't." And then: "Let me see."

Sure enough, she liked it! In fact, the following week, Mom let the chemical work its magic on her own legs and soon my younger sisters were also "Nairing" away.

The bus was nearly full when a young guy with a sweet face, chocolate brown eyes, and a medium build—wearing a letterman sweater—walked to the back with his friends and squished into a space next to me on that long seat. After a while he said, "Are you OK? Can I help you with anything?"

I shook my head, not making eye contact.

"Why don't you join us?" he said. "I'm John, a senior. My friends are Doug, Tom, and Terry. What's your name? You're new here, right?"

Soon, the dark cloud lifted, and I began to talk with them and enjoy the experience . . . even laughing. It was such a relief. When we arrived back at school, John offered to wait with me until my dad came to pick me up.

The next morning, I stood by myself among the crowd in the co-ed alley, the gathering place located between the boys' and girls' school. I waited for the flag raising and the reciting of the Pledge of Allegiance. I felt awkward, all alone, but confident that I would never again allow myself to be humiliated by those Mean Girls.

Soon John and his friends joined me.

"Doing better today?" they wanted to know.

"Much," I happily replied. They had come to my rescue. I could feel they genuinely cared about my welfare.

It wasn't long before the Mean Girls were all over me. "How do you know John? He's a popular senior."

"You're not dating him, are you?"

I felt a sense of victory. Not a total triumph, because it wasn't about me being accepted—just recognized, because I was noticed by John. I needed protection, I decided, from Mean Girls. I put on my first piece of armor that day. I would not be pierced in that way again.

THE PALACE

In the summer of 1963, Al, my boyfriend, and five of his friends rented a house in the Venice area. It was on a street off an alley called "the breezeway." We used to call these streets "the alphabet streets" back then because each street's name was in alphabetical order. The breezeway is south of Washington Blvd. and goes all the way to the Marina. These six guys named the house "The Palace" as it looked and felt like one. It was an old gray stone building on the corner of Fleet Street. The entrance opened right into a vast, empty living room. A lovely, aged, and elegant wrought-iron stairway curved up to the second-story landing, which overlooked the whole living area. There was not much in the way of furniture as bits and pieces were brought from the boys' parents' home to furnish the place. It remained rather cold, dark, and uncomfortable.

Eric Burton and the Animals had just recorded

the hit song "House of the Rising Sun" about a brothel. This summer haunt was the closest place to a house of ill repute that I was to witness. These boys were nineteen to twenty-one and they were typical guys . . . out to party and have a good time.

I was rather shocked and dismayed at the place the first time I visited. It was a Saturday morning and when someone walked into the "palace," it was obvious to them that there were women visitors and lots of beer bottles with ashtrays full of cigarette butts. I thought, "This was where my boyfriend was going to live?" "What was going on last night?"

We had been together the night before, but I was curious as to what he had come home to once he had dropped me off.

One Saturday evening started off rather innocuously. The guys threw a regular summer party for us all. They had hired a decent inexperienced band to play atop the landing and had ordered a couple kegs of beer. The news of the party traveled rapidly by mouth even without the help of the internet.

While throwing down some beers and dancing to this excellent live band one day, I became rather lost in the music and frivolity and the living room suddenly became way too crowded to even move and I felt as though I was being pushed around. There were hordes of people unknown to me outside and some even climbing in through the windows. Someone threw a chair into another window and a fight started. Al rushed me and some of the other girlfriends up the stairs to a bedroom and told us to stay there until they came back for us. We heard the band stop playing, glass breaking, screaming and yelling . . . basically a massive drunken brawl.

When Al returned with blood-covered knuckles, he grabbed my hand and said, *"Quick we need to leave, now!"*

Down the curved staircase we rushed to an almost empty house. There were sirens in the background and a few unconscious bodies sprawled out in front of the entrance to the "palace." Al quickly pulled me into the alley in order to avoid the police as the sirens hailed their menacing sounds. I was frightened and felt like I was in the movie *Rebel Without a Cause*! Here I was, young and out for a good time of fun and adventure, only to find myself in a shadowy and startling nightmare of sorts.

The sirens were getting louder with lights flashing on Washington as Al and I ducked into a back fence area to avoid the police and ambulances rushing toward the house. We needed to get away from there and to Al's car, which was parked on Washington Blvd.

I made it home safe without breaking my curfew.

My folks never knew that we had been a part of this incident, which was later reported on the news. It was all extremely electrifying, but I didn't think I wanted to attend another "palace" party.

While riding my bike on "the breezeway" a few months ago, I stopped to view the "palace." It's still an amazing old structure that's unchanged . . . the outside anyway. A man approached me and said, *"You won't see him today as he is out of town."*

With a puzzled look on my face, I asked, *"Who?"* and he replied, *"The owner, Johnny Rotten!"*

WOW I thought. Johnny Rotten of the Sex Pistols now owns the "palace"! I had this amazing thought . . . could he have been part of the outstanding band that played that evening in 1963 and had he come back to re-invent the "palace"?!

BROKEN

Broken bones are not fun but, in my case, they proved to be a thrilling adventure. Breaking my right leg led me to my first husband and the sport of snow skiing.

I was headed for June Mountain in the Sierras on a group bus trip. It was only my second time skiing, the first being a trip to Wrightwood in the San Bernardino Mountains for one day a few weeks earlier, and it had been a disaster. Taking the lift to the top of the mountain and having no idea how to handle skis, I had come down mostly on my butt and face and after being bruised and beaten both physically and mentally by this mountain, and ending up with a rip-roaring migraine.

"Never again," I told myself. "This sport is not for me."

So . . . how did I let myself get talked into this second ski trip and to a bigger and more challenging mountain range at that? A good friend asked me to go with her, and I don't know how to say no.

She had rented our skis, so I did not even get fitted correctly. The practically "bear claw" bindings on the skis were set for a beginner and that meant that they would release when I took a spill. For those of you not familiar with snow skiing, the bindings are just that . . . they bind your foot to the ski.

As we were loading up the bus with our equipment, someone said, "Hello" to my friend. His name was Carroll, and he was extremely handsome. He was tall and thin with dark blue eyes and a smile that lit his face up like the sun. DeDe introduced us. Carroll was the older brother of her boyfriend, Phil. Carroll sat in the seat in front of us and we talked for the whole seven-hour trip. At first it was the three of us who talked but then it was just Carroll and me. I think that is when I fell in love with him. We drank beer and ate chips and somewhat partied while discussing skiing and he asked the usual questions.

"How long have you been skiing?"

"Oh, you're new to the sport. Well, I'll help you get started in the morning."

He was true to his word. Carroll helped with my boots by tying the old-fashioned laces up nice and tight for a snug fit. Then he gave me some pointers and we got into the lift line and took the chair to the top.

On the way down the run, I fell plenty while doing giant snowplow turns, and each time the bindings snapped open and the skis popped off. Carroll was very patient with me but, even so, I suggested that he go and ski on his own while I continued to master the snowplow—an awkward position at best with knees bent together and skis splayed out with tips facing inward.

We met up for lunch in the lodge. I asked him to do a run with me once we were finished as I had practiced and was doing better. Before getting my skis back on, I had tightened the bindings so they wouldn't open so easily.

First run down the slope after lunch and, taking a few smooth wide turns with Carroll right behind me, I took a slow fall straight over the tips of my skis. The bindings did not release so both my bones above my right ankle broke just over the boot. Ouch! I felt nauseous. The pain was the worst physical pain I had ever experienced in my twenty years of life.

I was flat on the snow, face down, and with such a sharp pain shooting up from the break into my calf and knee with no feeling whatsoever in my foot. I looked back to make sure I still had a foot. There it was, attached to my leg and the ski that was now stuck in the snow. I didn't want to cry or yell out in front of Carroll so I just banged my fist into the snow and prayed that I would not pass out. Someone skied past and asked if we needed help. In about five minutes the ski patrol arrived, splinted my leg, and I rode down the hill in a basket with a spiral break of my tibia and fibula.

The next year, Carroll and I returned to June Mountain as a married couple. We were back on the slopes, only he was no longer as patient with me and took off with his friends to the top of the mountain and left me on my own. I was determined to learn to ski the right way with professional group lessons. And so began my love affair with skiing. As my love for this sport has lasted, I regretfully report that my marriage to Carroll did not.

A Life-Changing Moment

S he was looking back at me with those steely gray, omniscient, slanted eyes. Was she really mine?! The day before she lived in my imagination kicking and wriggling her way around inside of me . . . so close to entering the world.

Wendy had the softest wisp of blond fuzz cradling her sweetheart-shaped face, but it was the way she looked at me—a look that seemed to know me better then I knew myself, a look that was so penetrating and searching.

What was she thinking?

What did she know?

I had heard that babies cannot see much in those first days of their life, but they can hear and recognize voices. She looked up at the voice that she knew so well because I spoke to her constantly while in utero. Does living inside of you give them access to your feelings? Can they sense your fears, your joys, your anxieties? Can they sense you and therefore know you?

It was eight hours after Wendy was born that I was able to hold her like this for the first time, and as I unwrapped her from the tight, burrito-style pink blanket, I checked her out and made sure that she had all her little fingers and toes. Wendy was perfect. She was real, not a doll to play with as I envisioned, but a human girl child that could break and hurt, who would laugh and cry. And for eighteen years it would be up to me to shield her, guide her, and allow her to grow and thrive on her own one day. This moment was so humbling and frightening all at the same time—the latter because I now felt the monstrous responsibility I had taken on.

I loved Wendy more than life itself from that moment on. The loving part was easy. The mother-role part was immense as I was still a child myself in many ways, yearning to live and grow up unencumbered by the stress of the child-raising I was embarking on.

We began our lives together in that moment and my life was changed forever in the best possible way.

A Hot Wind

The wind roars like a lion and sucks the moisture from my skin; the heat drenches my body in prickly perspiration. I feel fear and dread from this Santa Ana wind. I once heard that *Santana* was what the Indians called this wind—Santana as in Satan, a more appropriate name. Some call this time of the year Indian Summer. . . . It's a pleasant title but not for me. Once this hot wind arrives, it brings on the pain of migraines and some sad memories.

There is something in this weather condition that triggers the onslaught of my horrendous headaches. The pain ascends from the back of my neck and, like a dark cloud, engulfs me and feels like an explosion of nails going off behind my eyes.

This blast affects my senses to light and sound, and I'm forced into my bedroom with shades pulled and a pillow wrapped around my head as I curl up into a fetal position, wanting and waiting for it to be over. If I can fall asleep it might end . . . unless the vomiting starts, and the agony continues.

These Santa Anas draw so much water out of the air that the photos I have attached to my refrigerator curl up. Walking outside is like being consumed by a furnace. The wind is so strong that it blows palm fronds across my path as I try to run on the Santa Monica bluffs. Unless this wind is at my back, it is like running in place. As I look out at the Pacific Ocean, I see an orange-brown film on the horizon.

These satanic winds usually bring fire and smoke and dread. My mother died during these winds. Fire was not far off, and the smoke had changed the color of the sky to an orange-yellow haze that gave the atmosphere an eerie otherworldliness, that matched the scene of my mother struggling for her last breaths.

Two years later my friend Michael died during these Satan winds as he lost his fight against cancer.

The memory that hurts me the most was a day in 1979 when the hot Santa Ana wind was howling, and tree branches were brushing against the dust-strewn windows of our home. The scratch, scratch of the leaves was like a drumroll of an execution. My migraine was building, and I had to tell my eleven-year-old daughter that her father and I were separating. She knew, I think, on some level, what was coming. I saw her jaw become set and her small, sweet face grow wary as I asked her to sit down with me.

"We need to talk," I said.

Her big dark blue eyes were already pooling with tears. I broke her heart that day, a heart I never thought I would be the one to break. It was on this day that the pain of my migraine was welcome because I felt I deserved to suffer. So let the vomiting begin.

TEARS

A veil of sorrow descended over me last week while I was in the theater to watch *The Art of Racing in the Rain*. This movie was so touching, and my heart was bursting with sadness and joy; only I found I couldn't cry.

Many, many years ago, around the time I was eight years old, I knew the tears must end. I wanted them to leave and never come back! As my small head rested on my crossed arms on my small school desk, hiding from the shame I was feeling, I made a pledge to myself to block the tears. I fought for this with everything in my being. I would feel them coming on and inside my head scream, "No, NO, **NO!**"

I wasn't successful at first. Those pesky tears would flow regardless of how hard I tried to stop them. Embarrassment, shame, and fear of rejection would force them out of my eyes. I was ridiculed at home and especially at school by my classmates.

"Laurie is such a crybaby!" they would chant.

It seemed I, so insecure of myself in front of others that my mind would go blank, was the first one to misspell a word in a class spelling bee. I would get perfect scores for written spelling tests, but standing in front of the classroom would bring such terror to me that I couldn't think straight.

They could predict the tears when I missed a word and start laughing, pointing at me and saying,

"There she goes again!"

I was mortified. I hated these tears.

At home, my mom would tell me to stop crying when I was hurt either physically or emotionally. Falling and skinning my knees would find me running to Mom, crying.

"Stop crying or I won't clean off your knees!" was her response.

I remember, with heaving breaths, trying to stop the tears from cascading down my face. Tears must be dark and awful, I thought, as nobody liked them. I worked and worked on getting rid of them.

By high school I was in better control of them. I felt weak when I cried and hated that feeling so I persuaded myself to reject them even more.

As time moved on, and I was in my twenties, it seemed easier to control the tears. People would comment to me: "You're so stoic!"

Miraculously, I realized one day that the tears were gone. I had a hard time crying.

When watching a sad movie or reading a book, if I was by myself, the tears would come and it felt so good. I realized that what I so disliked about the tears was the scorn I would receive. By myself I could cry without being made fun of.

This very natural and cathartic human function had been wiped out!

I had done a job on myself. Even when I was by myself with no one to view my tears, I would not let them flow . . . like in this movie. A cold, steel wall drops in my psyche to prevent the feelings in my heart from traveling anywhere near my head and tear ducts. My body has learned to automatically stop this function and I caused this. That is a result and darkness that I could not have foretold. The last time I really cried was when my father died in 2000.

My daughter, Wendy, cried a lot when she was little for all kinds of reasons—being scolded, being afraid, being hurt emotionally. Oh, God, how she reminded me of me! By twenty-two I was already fairly shut down. I knew it to be a problem. I loved Wendy's tears and did not want her to be ashamed of them. I defended her crying jags to her father and teachers.

"She's just overly sensitive," I would tell others, and I would hold her and tell her it was OK to cry and that I treasured her tears. Wendy is now fifty-one and still can cry easily—big, quiet tears roll down her cheeks as she shares her pain. How lucky she is!

Unknowingly I've turned myself into an ice queen, unable to show hurt of sad feelings. The damage I performed on myself was profound and is so dark and awful that I am now embarrassed and ashamed for not being able to cry.

No More Tears
by Laurie Forrest

The tears are gone . . .
Permanently?
Who knows?

They have disappeared, dried up,
evaporated!

I wanted the tears to go
and never come back

Once sweet and salty,
bringing relief from
pain and hurt.

It used to be easy.
Too easy, perhaps.

The tears became a burden . . . and plagued me.

Teasing and ridicule
the result of tears appearing
. . . wetting my face.

Why these tears were shameful was a testimony
to how cruel society can be on a child.

RUNNING FOR MY LIFE

I knew when I was nine years old. Glued to the TV screen and watching the games, I knew I wanted to compete in the Olympics as a runner. In grammar school I could outrun all the girls in my class, in every grade, and even beat the fastest boys. I was a natural and I loved it. Running gave me confidence and self-esteem. But no one really noticed me or acknowledged my ability. There were no cross-country or track-and-field competitions for girls. And I soon lost interest.

But my passion for running was rekindled in the middle 1960s. Before work in the mornings, I would throw on a T-shirt and shorts, lace up my tennis sneakers, and head out for a jog in my neighborhood. It felt great until one foggy morning a car with three boys yelled out the window: "Hey, dyke!"

I wasn't even sure what the slur meant back then but I had an idea. I stopped running. I guess it was not the lady-like thing to do.

Running was just in my blood and I couldn't resist, so I started back up after I was married. It was a whole new experience. I was amazed as it seemed like the world had caught up with me. More women were out jogging, giving me permission to run all I wanted! It felt glorious—the wind against my face and rustling through my hair; the warmth that travels up my legs and into my arms and torso. I could feel God's pleasure as I ran, giving me a sense that I could do anything.

In a few years' time, I heard of a 10K race being held in Brentwood and signed up for it. My husband and I had been out drinking the night before, had gotten in late, and now here it was: the painful morning after.

"All you need is a couple cups of coffee to get you going," suggested my husband.

So, with determination and a half pot of coffee, I made it to the starting line surprised at the hundreds of people there pumping up, stretching their calves and hamstrings, while I wished to feel better. To make matters worse, it was a very hot day, and the race began late. I really wanted my first competitive run to be significant, but here I was dehydrated and feeling like shit. I even wet my pants toward the end of this 6.2-mile run. Somehow, I managed to finish, but I wondered: *What did I do wrong?*

From then on, I started reading about how to race. I learned about hydrating, carb loading, training properly, and wearing a good running shoe—Nikes were just showing up in the marketplace.

I became a true runner. I started winning medals in the 5 and 10K races I signed up for. I joined the Santa Monica Track Club, acquired lasting friends, and soon was doing half marathons. Finally, I signed up for the 1988 LA Marathon at age forty-two.

The gun went off!

Could I do this?

Two friends joined me to support my running the first half.

I was wearing a tank top from Santa Monica Track Club with the bold letters SMTC on the front in the hopes of staying relatively cool throughout the race.

The excitement of the start and all the spectators cheering for us propelled me on. I found many of the supporters lining the route were children who had their hands out for high-fives. I would run over to the sidelines and touch their hands and one gave me a balloon to carry. As we ran my other friend, Angie, who had run a marathon before, warned me to conserve my energy as I would eventually run out of steam.

"Stay focused on the run and slow down" was her advice.

Angie and Leslie left me at mile twelve. By then I was feeling the pain and lack of energy coming on and became worried that I would not be able to finish. Getting to mile thirteen was difficult.

Then I saw my mom, dad, and sisters—Gerry and Eileen—and that perked me up. Eileen jumped into the race next to me and fed me orange slices that my mom had brought. At this point I had slowed down a bit and enjoyed this treat. Eileen left me at mile fourteen and by mile fifteen I had gotten a second wind. I was able to cruise through the next six miles.

They say you "hit the wall" at mile twenty, which means that you have nothing left. For me, it was mile twenty-one. At this mile, Larry jumped into the race. As he ran next to me, he commented: *"This is easy!"* I wanted to smack him, only I didn't have the energy. He lasted one mile.

It was such a surreal experience, this last part of the course. The bottoms of my feet would burn each time my foot struck the pavement. I was sure I was loaded with blisters. My legs did not want to move. What an odd feeling to not be able to have my legs move automatically. My brain had to talk them through; each leg had to be coaxed to lift and step forward. By mile twenty-five, I had to walk while continuing to speak to my legs.

Three young Black boys must have seen that I was fading fast. They called out, "Hey SMTC, you can do it!" and held out their hands. I walked over to them and slapped each of their upturned hands and looked into their sweet smiling faces . . . and started to run that last mile.

My thought: *If these little guys believe I can do it, then I can!"*

The supporters lining that last mile brought me in. In that crowd were Angie and Leslie as well as my folks, sisters, and Larry. I could hear each of them hollering my name. I knew that I would make it!

Crossing that finish line four hours and twenty minutes after starting the race was ecstasy! Once I received my medal, I walked aways to the restroom. Hooray, I didn't have blood in my urine, a good sign. Then I removed my shoes and socks. NO blisters . . . amazing! I walked on the cool grass, carrying my shoes, and went looking for my family and friends. My spirits were soaring, and I remained in this state of euphoria for weeks after.

If I could run a marathon, I could do anything! was my thinking.

Two weeks ago, I was one of the spectators helping to bring in those running this year's LA marathon. I know I reached at least five of these participants. They were dragging; I knew how they felt. I caught their eye while clapping and screamed: "You can do this! Looking good! Almost there!" They smiled, perked up a bit, and mouthed, "Thank you!"

I missed my chance as an Olympic hopeful but my daughter didn't. Wendy came close. I lived vicariously through her achievements as I watched her run competitively in high school and compete in state meets. She made varsity at CAL in cross-country and the 800 meters in track and field. Wendy realized by her second year of college that she had reached her peak and was not going to pursue the Olympics. She continued varsity her remaining two years at CAL, and now does long-distance running just for her own delight. I now watch my granddaughters, nine and twelve and endowed with the same athletic skills for running, winning medals of their own.

I always wondered whether, if I had been born at a different time, or gone to a different high school, I could have been an Olympic contender. Recently I have had to stop jogging entirely due to a back injury. I realize that this sport defined me, and I am left with a sadness and longing that I still deal with.

My running turned out to be a real-life dream. It brought me joy and happiness, helped me through bad times, guided me to my career in nutrition and a way to support myself, and made me strong. I didn't really need to be in the Olympics.

FRAGILE

I raced from the restroom and right into his arms! "I didn't hurt you, did I?"

He flashed me his most exuberant smile: "No . . . it's my pleasure!"

If I had it planned, it could not have worked out this well. I was a fan and was there to see him run. And finding myself in the arms of Steve Prefontaine, the famous distance runner of the 1970s, was such a delightful experience. Running was a new sport for me, and Steve Prefontaine, known as Pre, was my idol.

This chance encounter with him happened in 1974, where he was running the 2,000-meter race at the Sunkist Invitational Indoor Meet being held at the Los Angeles Sports Arena.

Steve was warming up in the foyer area where the washrooms were located, and I wanted to make sure that I was in the stands as his event was about to start. And that is how I stumbled into him.

Once the race began and I was seated, I truly enjoyed watching his long, dark blond scruffy hair fly off his face as he raced, and his svelte body with those long legs that carried him to the finish line was a wonder to behold as we all hollered: "Pre, Pre, Pre!!" A chant that rocked the stadium!

He came in first, and it was a brilliant run. It sure looked like he was ready for the '76 Olympics in Montreal.

Watching Steve run was an incentive for me to get up early and put on my shoes and sweats each morning. This form of exercise made me feel on the inside as glorious as Steve looked on the outside.

Steve had been training for these Olympic games hoping to prove that he could beat Lasse Viren of Finland, who had won the 5,000-meter event in 1972. In that race, Prefontaine, after being boxed in, a position he abhorred, pulled out into the lead for a good portion of the race, running an excellent pace, but he was passed up in the last lap by Viren and two others, to come in fourth place. He was devastated and depressed, and even considered hanging up his running shoes.

The backdrop to these Olympics were the Munich massacre of the Israeli weightlifters—a few days of terror that erupted before our eyes on television, Steve watching from the building across the way. It was not a good way to mentally prepare for an Olympic event that might not even take place. But it did and he ran his best.

Unlike many European nations who back in those days paid their athletes to run, Pre had to work at night so he could train by day. His coach, Bill Bowerman, was designing a better running shoe for his team by creating a different tread using his wife's waffle iron. Steve could have made a fortune as the model for the new Nike shoe, but then he would not have been able to compete in the Olympics as he would lose his amateur status.

Steve was twenty-four years old in May of 1975, just one year after my wonderful run-in with him. He died driving into a rock wall, flipping his little yellow sports car at 2 in the morning after working as a bartender.

What a vital sports figure he was to me and the US. A running icon who I'd tried to emulate was gone. He had been someone I followed in the paper and magazines, watched on TV, and fantasized about. Steve, whose VO2 max (maximal oxygen uptake) was off the charts, would never take another breath.

This memory recalls feelings that have come over me recently about the fragility of life.

My brother, Mark, and his family were evacuated from their home in Santa Rosa due to the fires in that area. The worry I felt dangled over me as the smoke hung over Northern California.

My godson and his wife attended the Route 91 Harvest Music Festival in Las Vegas. They were so excited to celebrate their anniversary in this way but found themselves running to get away from a gunman, seeing others being shot around them. Once they found shelter, they saw that they were covered in others' blood. They were safe but are having the equivalent of PTSD and survivors' remorse.

These reminders of how quick our sense of life can change are the realities that face us each day. We just never know when something like death, whether it be by car, fire, or gunshot, will happen.

As I view the poster of Steve that I have hanging in my room, a picture of him finishing up a race, I remember his famous quote: "To give anything less than your best is to sacrifice the gift."

I am working on living more in the moment, having gratitude for each day, and giving my best.

THE VISIT

There was a knock at my apartment door. It was my neighbor Larry, asking if I had four quarters for a dollar as he was doing laundry. He had a glass of wine in his hand. He patiently waited at my front door while I dug out the change he needed. Then . . .

"Would you like to join me for a glass of wine? It's quite good. I just opened this bottle of Cabernet before doing laundry and thought you might like to join me."

There I was in my white terrycloth robe; Wendy (my daughter) was working on an essay for school while I was studying for a biochemistry test the next day.

"No; maybe another night when Wendy is not with me."

"Well . . . what night is good for you?"

"Mondays," I replied.

A few weeks before, I had met Larry briefly in the elevator while rushing to get my daughter off to school. In the ride down to the garage, he was particularly personable, introducing himself and charming Wendy. As we climbed into "Charlie," my 1973 powder blue VW Bug, the following conversation ensued:

Wendy: "He's cute, Mom."
Me: "He is, and too young for me."
Wendy: "He has the same wrinkles around his eyes as you do."

It had been a tough year for me. Once my husband Carroll and I separated, I found the whole dating scene had changed significantly from the early '60s to the late '70s, and I wasn't handling it very well. So, I made a conscious choice to not go out with anyone for a full year and just learn to be content on my own. God knows I had enough on my plate working full time, going to school, and being a single mom.

Looking back, it was the year of truly finding myself. Instead of waiting for another person to decide the future, I explored what it was that I wanted to do. I took trips on my own; and, together, Wendy and I planned outings. On weekends we visited Los Angeles museums and amusement parks, took long walks on the beach, and dined out. I did not miss having a man in my life. I found things to be a lot less complicated.

Once the year was up, my girlfriends started bugging me: "It is time you started dating again."

"When I am meant to meet someone, he will come knocking at my door," I replied.

That was Larry's visit . . . a month later! I would see Larry on the Santa Monica Bluffs running and we decided shortly after that first visit to do a run on a Monday evening and then go to dinner. What fun he was to be with—easy to talk to, funny, smart, cute. He shared with me that he had a girlfriend who he spent time with on the weekends. I liked his honesty, and at that point, I think I became even more attracted to him.

How convenient, I thought: A boy who was a friend and neighbor and I could foresee no entanglements.

From then on, Monday nights were ours! He became my "boy-toy," and I was "Monday night Laurie" to his circle of friends. This lasted a year . . . until we both became more heavily invested in the relationship.

Eventually the girlfriend left, and Larry and I became a couple, slowly merging into each other's social lives but liking our separate homes and ways.

Once Wendy was immersed in college and

deciding that Berkeley was where she wanted to live and work, Larry and I decided to share our household. Since he had the bigger unit, I moved in there. Our joint relationship was together but somewhat disconnected. It was like we were in the doldrums.

I had always wanted to try living in a different city. I had wanted it with Wendy's father when she was young. We drove that six-hour trip to Mammoth every other weekend. He hated his job. Why not move to Colorado where snow skiing would be much more accessible? But there was no way he would move. Larry also had no desire to move out of Santa Monica.

Wendy was living in Berkeley and loving it. I wanted to give it a try. Soon the opportunity presented itself with a job offer in Monterey, CA. This became another year of self-discovery: Being on my own in another city; finding a place to live and my way around town; making new friends; and discovering a life outside of Southern California. Being closer geographically to Wendy, I could partake in her college experience and on weekends we explored the joys of Northern California.

Although Larry and I would spend time together each month, I missed his sweetness on a more regular basis and in time we recognized the importance of what we had. This temporary job ended.

I moved back to Santa Monica and, as the saying goes, the rest is history.

Seventeen years after that innocuous knock at my door, we married. And so, thirty-five years ago this month, I celebrate the visit that changed my life.

FIRE

I t was October of 1991, and I was driving home to Monterey after spending a sweet weekend with Larry. Although we were living apart, we managed to spend at least two weekends a month together. This separation was what truly brought us together and into the awareness that we maybe should be in a more committed relationship.

I loved these solitary drives in my little blue VW bug, the windows open, letting the ocean breeze cool down the hot dry air inside, blasting my cassette tapes so I could hear the tunes over the traffic noise. My routine was to drive north on PCH to the 101 and get past Santa Barbara, where I had to really watch my speed. The tickets were expensive, and I would be unable to make it up in traffic school. I already had two speeding tickets from these trips to and from LA.

Next stop, Santa Inez or Solvang, where I stopped for gas, a bite, and a bathroom. Once I got to San Luis Obispo, I'd reached my halfway point. Not much traffic from there on in and it was open country and beautiful that time of day—around 2:30 p.m.—especially coming down 101 into King City.

The land glittered as if pixie dust had been sprinkled over it. I was singing along with Billy Joel to "She's Always a Woman," my short hair blowing around my face, remembering my pleasurable time with Larry.

Unbeknownst to me was that my daughter, Wendy, was having one of the worst days of her life and needed me. It was Sunday morning of the 20th and she and her boyfriend at the time, Andrew, had taken an early morning run in the Berkeley Hills. Andrew drove them both back to Oakland where Wendy and her roommate Holly lived. There was smoke—lots of it—close to her apartment.

"Holly, wake up!" Wendy screamed as she gathered up her car keys, wallet, some clothes, and her pictures.

Wendy told me that Holly was asleep, and as she woke up, said: "What's going on?"

She opened the drapes to the patio, and they both watched the beginning of the Tunnel Fire flying down the hill and starting to burn their apartment.

Wendy panicked as she saw this and dropped what she had in her arms and ran down the hall, hitting the fire alarms with Holly and Andrew close behind as they raced to their cars. While they each drove separately down the narrow Caldecott Tunnel, they passed the fire engines on their way up. They are the only three who got their cars out. Others in the Parkwood Apartments had to flee on foot as the fire trucks blocked the road. Holly and Wendy met at Andrew's apartment across from the Claremont Hotel and watched on TV as their apartment building burned to the ground.

Those damn Diablo winds, cousins to our Santa Anas or "devil winds," as I like to call them. She didn't die like twenty-five others in that devastating fire. And her apartment complex was one of over 3,000 structures that burned to the ground that day. But it was earth shattering for her. She had nightmares for years after . . . always being chased by fire.

I got home about six o'clock the night of the twentieth, and there were fifteen messages on my answering machine. *Oh, my, that's strange as I never get that many phone calls.* The first two were from Wendy and she was sobbing. "I've lost every-thing, Mom!"

I could taste the bile in my throat as my heart raced. Yikes!! What was happening? The next five messages told me that she was safe and at Andrew's.

"Mom, call me, please!"

Now I turned on the television and on every news-station was fire—the firestorm in Oakland. I watched as I listened to the rest of the messages. She was telling me that they were being evacuated from Andrew's apartment. Holly's folks called to let me know Wendy was OK. Andrew's mother wanted me to know that they were all at their home waiting to get word that they could go back to Andrew's apartment. Carroll, Wendy's dad, left two messages that she was scared but safe.

By then I was feeling rather punky. I was bliss-fully driving home without a care in the world and her world was burning down. I called as soon as I retrieved the last message hoping that, by then, they were back at Andrew's. Wendy had calmed down but cried about all that she had lost. She didn't even have a toothbrush or a change of underwear . . . only the running clothes on her back.

The following weekend, Holly's mom, Sally, flew from Boise to San Francisco and we met her there. We shopped that whole weekend, outfitting them. The girls shared their stories of the escape and Sally and I chatted about how we'd found out what was going on.

Wendy no longer had much attachment to things. "They can burn," she informed me in that cold way of someone who'd been hurt.

She had been applying to different colleges for entrance into a master's program. They wanted samples of her writing. However, when they heard everything was lost in the Tunnel Fire, no more questions were asked.

For years, when she was reminded of what was missing, she would cry.

"Hey, Honey," I'd say. "Let's go through your baby book." And, crying, she would reply, "It's gone." I kept forgetting.

I've heard that every cloud has a silver lining. Wendy received funds due to the disaster. She used them for her master's degree in Irish literature from Trinity College in Dublin. This was a new adventure for her and wasn't something that could burn.

Michael

The last time I saw Michael was September 2009. We ran three miles together, very slowly, and with intermittent walking. He was fatigued. He was dying. Michael had been fighting a melanoma "the size of a Big Mac" in his gut and the melanoma had finally won out.

Michael knew it was a death sentence when he was diagnosed the year before, but he wanted time. More time with his daughter. It was her last year of high school, and he was hoping to know which college she would attend. Mostly he loved life and did not want to leave it.

We were the same age. He was effervescent—lovely green eyes with a glint of mischief in them, smiling like he was about to crack a witty remark. We ran together every Saturday morning for the last ten years. I think I loved him from the first time we met when Ray, a fellow runner, asked him to join our jogging group.

How do I explain this puzzling sense that happens when I meet a stranger for the first time but recognize them as familiar. Since I dabble in reincarnation, I sometimes think when this happens that the person and I were together in a past life and that they were someone special. A wise friend once told me that when God, a big blob of love, kept expanding, It was so tickled with itself it soon exploded. The pieces were strewn all over the universe and when you meet someone you know, it could be that he was the God piece right next to your God piece, like a puzzle that will fit together and complete a picture! Sounds terribly esoteric, I know, but that's how I felt about Mike—as though we were connected from the get-go.

Still, we were different in ways: a conservative republican versus a liberal democrat; an agnostic versus a believer. But there was a notable link between us.

I marveled at how he never missed a run.

"What I love about our run on Saturday mornings is that it's the one day of the week that I forget I'm dying of cancer; I feel happy."

Mike shared this with me toward the end of his life. He would wait on the Bluffs overlooking the Pacific—just gazing longingly as if for the last time. Once aware of my footsteps behind him, he would open his arms and greet me with his generous warm smile and enfold me in his arms—and off we would go to join the rest of the gang.

Our group met at San Vicente and Ocean and, once together, we let him call the shots.

"Let's shuffle," Mike would say; translated, this meant the slowest of jogs.

Along with running, my group of friends would celebrate our birthdays together over breakfast. Since Michael would forever be sixty- four, I looked at my birthday in a whole new way:

Wow, I get to be seventy! is how I think now, instead of: *"Yikes, I'm getting so old.*

When approaching Palisades Park now to do my workout, I picture him leaning up against the stone railing, studying the view. I see him turn and walk toward me with his wide-open arms. He is still with me.

FERRIS WHEEL

I t was August in Boise 2006. The summer heat was in the nineties and had a parched, valley hotness to it. There was finally a breeze and what a delightful relief from the scorch of the sun as I sweated and felt sucked dry by the hot spell. I looked to the sky, and was caught in awe by the brilliant orange and pink light coming from the setting sun through wispy clouds covering the powder-blue sky while enjoying the smells of barbecued chicken and roasted corn. It was noisy, with children's laughter and squeals and the whir, whir, whirring of carnival rides as we waited in the seemingly endless line to ride the Ferris wheel at the Idaho State Fair. This would be the last queue before we packed it up and went home.

Audrey, my granddaughter, who had just turned four, came up to her Mommy and me and said:

"I want to go too! I am not afraid.". . . as she clung to my leg.

She'd decided she'd rather ride the Ferris wheel with us than stay on the sidelines with her daddy and papa.

Audrey had to be tired as we had been at the fair since just before noon, and by then it was around nine at night. Wisps of her thin blond hair were stuck to her sticky cheeks from the pink cotton candy she had eaten earlier, and dirt smudges stained her small round face. The braids that we'd worked on so diligently that morning were slowly coming undone. She had been like a little jumping bean, unable to stand still for a moment. And those enormous, deep, steel-blue eyes looked up at us with such merriment. Wendy, her mother, and I explained that once she was on the Ferris wheel, she could not get off.

Audrey nodded her understanding; she was committed, and it showed through her nervous excitement.

Finally, our turn arrived, and Audrey bravely marched along, looking so grown up as she climbed aboard. The Ferris wheel crept to the top as it let out and took in new passengers. As it approached, Audrey caught her breath and grabbed onto my arm; the twinkle of new stars appeared in the darkening sky, and then, whoosh, the wheel started to descend with some speed toward the crowd.

Her face was radiant with a big smile as we got ready for the second spin. "I like it!" she yelled.

When the ride slowed down and Audrey's giggles filled my ears, we got off and she jumped into my arms with such exuberance and said: "I DID IT, Nana! I DID it!"

I remembered being there . . . right where she was . . . so willing to experience something but being afraid. Wanting an experience so much that I was willing to take the fear with me and continue. Witnessing her joy made me wonder if there were points in my life when I'd decided not to pursue certain pleasures due to being scared.

I liked to think that I mainly followed Audrey's example and enjoyed the thrills as well as the pain in doing so. I discovered successes, like the exhilaration of completing a marathon and receiving a master's degree. Jumping into a relationship with Larry for sex to find it developing into much more. But then there were the failures: a marriage gone sour, a destructive love affair along the way. Just like the ups and downs of the Ferris wheel.

Was I missing out now because of my dread? Did I have one too many events that were hurtful, disappointing, or just not worth the effort? Could it be an age thing? As I got older, I worried about the consequences more than ever before—the "what ifs," like speaking in front of a group, being vulnerable on the page, or breaking a leg. Some of my concerns were justified with maturity, but how often did I miss out on other life adventures because of my trepidation?

So, a beautiful sunset reminded me to take a new leap occasionally—like Audrey did that evening on the Ferris wheel.

KATHERINE

"*A*re you going to die soon, Nana?"

Katherine asked me this as I sat next to her in the back seat of their gray Forester, heading west toward a Sunday brunch at her other grandparents' home.

"I hope not!" I reply.

This was about the fifth time Katherine has asked me this question since I stepped off the plane in Boise, Idaho, just two days ago. I looked at her little face—those big, expressive brown eyes were questioning, and her forehead was crinkled up in anxiety. Now I was worried. Three years old is too young to be a little "worry heart" like this. I had to think of an answer to give her so that she wouldn't agonize so much.

Let me tell you about little Katherine: She is spunky and has a mind and style all her own. Dressing her can be so frustrating because she won't let you help her. She wants to do it her way.

I try to talk her out of it . . . but "no go." Once she is finished dressing, I want to run the other way or pretend she doesn't belong to me because she looks every bit the ragamuffin. Stretch pants with a skirt on and then a pair of shorts over the skirt, then on the top, a blouse, a T-shirt, and a dress to top it off. Of course, I cannot comb her hair either. I would never have let my daughter, Wendy, leave the house looking like that. However, Wendy tells me that Katherine is experiencing and expressing her own style. Boy, I'll say! I wonder if Wendy thinks I stifled her style. Well, that's for another story . . . now back to Katherine's worries about me dying.

Once we arrive at Katherine's other grandparents' home, I asked her Grandma Barbara if Katherine asked Grandpa Bob and her this question about dying. Barbara replied:

"Yes, all the time, ever since your mom died last year."

My mom was eighty-eight years old when she died, and she had the most beautiful gray/white hair. All of Katherine's little life, she heard that her Great Nana Vera, whom her mother loved very much, had cancer and was going to die. Her Grandpa Bob also has mostly gray hair tied back in a ponytail. And now my hair is becoming quite gray, since I am no longer coloring it. Barbara and I think that Katherine is associating our gray hair and wrinkles with someone who is old and might be dying soon. In fact, that would make perfect sense to a three-year-old. Katherine probably thinks that her mommy and daddy are old; but they don't have gray hair yet and are certainly not as wrinkled as us.

I remember as a little girl of six thinking that my grandparents were ancient. They certainly moved like someone who was old. My grandma using a cane to walk . . . Grandpa wore suspenders . . . and both had gray hair. That sort of meant a very old person to me.

While tucking her into her bed later that evening, she asked the question once again:

"Nana, are you going to die soon?"

This is what I told her:

"Katherine, my plan (and hopefully God approves) is to live to be ninety-two years old, and by then you will be thirty-four years old, and I will have held a few of your babies in my arms."

Katherine jumped up all excited and her eyes lit up.

"That old, Nana?" And I said:

"That's my plan, honey!"

And that was the last time I heard that question from her. Katherine is now eight. Oh . . . and she does have a fine sense of style and remains as feisty as ever!

Syd

The summer of 2014 was our family's time together at our casita in Abiquiu, New Mexico. My daughter Wendy and her husband, Darren, along with our two granddaughters, Audrey and Katherine, drove from Boise, Idaho, while Larry and I flew into Santa Fe from Los Angeles and rented a large white van that could fit the lot of us once we were all together.

We had lots of adventures on this trip: horseback riding at Ghost Ranch through that authentic Western setting; kayaking on Abiquiu Lake, which was so refreshing on a scorching hot day; an archery tournament that all had fun competing in. The trip through the paleontology museum was a chance for the girls to brush off silt from a tiny dinosaur.

However, the most memorable event happened the day our children arrived. We had dinner waiting for them after that long and tiring journey. And that was the night we met Syd. After dinner, the six of us were watching the children's movie *Caroline* when Larry went outside to look at the stars, and there it was—*rattle, Rattle, RATTLE!* Larry quickly did the Michael Jackson moonwalk back inside the door. Yes, our guest was a baby rattlesnake curled up on our portal just outside the front door. It was quite a loud rattle for a little guy. And what a blessing—as it saved Larry from stepping on it.

Oh, dear, our son-in-law Darren's greatest nightmare had come true. Before the trip he kept asking whether we would see a rattlesnake. *Was it safe for his girls?* Until then, we had never seen one, but we knew of others who had. Now it was our turn to deal with a rattler on our property. The girls named our baby snake, who was the color of slate with intermittent light yellow-brown colors weaving around his shiny body, Syd. Darren couldn't sleep. He worried all night about how to handle this dangerous little critter who had moved from the front door into another corner of our portal and curled up into a ball for the night. Syd could have been mistaken for a sizable rock had we not known he had slithered to that spot.

The next morning Darren was up at the crack of dawn on the computer checking Google for "what to do" with rattlesnakes. He then made calls around town to ask how to get rid of Syd, and was told, *Get a shovel, chop off the head, and then burn it.*

This was something Darren could not do. Darren is a vegetarian because he loves animals. He will not wear leather shoes or belts and carries a Velcro cloth wallet. While not fond of snakes, he does not believe in killing them. None of us wanted to do that to Syd.

Larry and Darren put on long-sleeve shirts and work gloves, grabbed a black plastic trash container from the utility closet, and found some longish, narrow tree branches to gently ease Syd into this trash can, while us girls safely watched through the windows inside our casita. Once they'd coaxed the snake in, the boys drove out five miles and then let him go free. For the rest of the week, we did not encounter another snake and enjoyed the great outdoors worry free. Darren may have continued to be troubled about possibly meeting a relative of Syd's but he did not bring the subject up.

Finding and relocating Syd was a highlight on this trip, and we all remember and laugh about it today. Whenever we visit our Casita, Darren and the girls ask, "Have you seen Syd?"

We have not, or any of his relatives!

ANNIE

Ann was popular and outgoing. At 5'5" with light brown, almost blond hair and lovely, large green eyes, she overshadowed my 5' small, flat frame. I was quiet, extremely young looking, didn't shave my legs yet, was a new student in this my sophomore year, and was not socially desired. We were both attending St. Monica High School in Santa Monica in the early sixties. Ann had attended St. Monica's since first grade and knew most everyone.

We had a few classes together and soon an attraction developed. For me, I became devoted to her. I admired her confidence and effervescent personality. I envied her popularity. She was not afraid to show off while I, on the other hand, did not want to be noticed. Yet she saw me and invited a friendship between us. I was surprised and overjoyed. I always assumed that she was the giver in our relationship only to discover that she thought it was the other way around. She recently shared that I was the only one that truly listened and accepted her for all that she was.

Life is curious—it's all about how we interpret it. She liked in me what I didn't like about myself at the time—being a quiet and unpopular, mostly terrified girl. She was smart, and I thought I wasn't. I had to work harder for my mediocre grades whereas it seemed to me that she aced many of the tests without a lot of studying. Later in our relationship Ann shared how she admired my discipline—getting an advanced degree all on my own while raising my daughter in comparison to her not finishing her second year of college in order to become an American Airlines flight attendant

Annie introduced me to books. I guess you could say that we became my first book club. We were both sexually curious. *The End of the Affair* by Graham Greene was the first book we read—her choice. After school, we would walk over to her home on 16th Street and Carlyle and read to each other, sitting cross-legged on her bed, and ruminate about certain sexual passages, imagining what sex would be like. Book reading became my new enthusiasm.

At school there were financial and social lines drawn. For example, if you lived north of Wilshire Blvd., you were considered wealthy and socially upper-class. Living south of Wilshire deemed you as poor and not part of the in-crowd. Annie lived in Santa Monica, north of Wilshire, and I lived in Venice, very south of Wilshire.

That didn't seem to matter to Ann. She turned sixteen, and got her license, a 1956 blue and white Chevy convertible sedan, and a gas credit card. I took the RTD bus to school and walked even to my part-time job at Jerry Brill's, a dress shop on Third Street in Santa Monica before it was the Promenade. However, once Ann got her license and car, she started driving each day to pick me up for school.

Recently when I mentioned to her how kind she was to me, she laughed, saying: "Laurie, I just loved driving and wanted an excuse to drive more. Picking you up was a win-win for us both!"

When we both graduated in 1963, Annie went off to the University of Hawaii and I stayed in town, worked, married, and had a baby girl. We had promised to stay in touch; however, the baby announcement I mailed to her was returned "addressee unknown." Years went by until I ran into her father at the Sears in Santa Monica while shopping with my daughter, Wendy, who was three years old.

"How is Annie?" I asked.

"She is here visiting us. Give me your number and I'll have her call you."

Later that evening, Ann called. "Laurie, I can't believe you're a mother!"

And we started yakking like no time had gone by. Later that evening, she came over to meet Wendy and see my home in Mar Vista.

Ann was engaged to a pilot living in Sebastopol, Northern California. Once married, she and her husband moved to El Rito, New Mexico. She bred and trained the most incredible Australian shepherd dogs before her four children arrived while her husband, David, was flying. She had a milking cow named "Mama Rose," raised pigs that she couldn't wait to eat, canned tomatoes and fruit, and had become "Ms. Granola," as she grew and made everything from scratch . . . including their adobe home along with her husband. I visited regularly—the city girl and country girl still sharing their lives and dreams over the years.

We have sat on her bed and discussed the pain of divorce and the trials and tribulations our children were going through. She eventually traded in her cows and pigs to sell real estate in the Land of Enchantment, and Larry and I bought our lovely casita from her.

We laugh now about how we used to talk about sex, how inquisitive we were about what it would be like, to now, being in our seventies and having it all behind us as well as grandchildren older than we were at the time.

In June of 2014, Ann and I got together in Abiquiu, New Mexico, with our children and grandchildren for a week. Her two grandchildren are the same ages as my two and they spent time at Ghost Ranch. They made movies on their iPhones and tried to swim in the very cold Abiquiu Lake. Annie and I had to pinch ourselves to be able to share our grandkids like this.

Recently my granddaughter Audrey, while at dinner with me in Boise, asked:

"How did Granny Annie and you stay together from high school to now?"

You see she is off to College in Oregon this summer and is worried she will lose touch with her best friend, Sophia.

I told her:

"You will have no problems keeping in touch with Sophia . . . as you have the internet, smartphones, and FaceTime—things that were not available to us. We had only letter writing and expensive long-distance phone calls, AND a great love and joy for each other."

Annie is a sincere friend! We have longevity together. We have time and space between us that doesn't affect the friendship. Months can go by without talking to one another and yet there is no dismay—only delight, in sharing time together when we do talk. We pick up where we left off. This is my definition of a true and loving relationship.

Annie is my friend and my true north—or, as my granddaughters say, my BFF, meaning Best Friends Forever!

HOMELESSNESS

I never felt homeless . . . until now.

"Should I stay or should I go?" This Clash tune was echoing in my head.

There was an overwhelming sense of disaster bubbling up within me. I had read many books on WWII and the Holocaust and had always had much gratitude for this land, and our freedoms.

"That could never happen here!" I thought. But lately I felt like this country was the "home of the corrupt" and the "land of the rich." That a man like Donald Trump could be running for president was horrifying but even more so was the fact that so many of my fellow citizens had voted for him. This made me feel as though I was an alien in a strange land. How did intelligent people vote for this narcissistic person who had no political experience and so much hatred and bigotry in his heart? I happened to know and love some of these people who thought he was the answer and was so angry at their ignorance that I wanted to scream; but then they felt the same toward me and my political views.

"Should I stay, or should I go?" England chose to go.

"Britain will never leave the EU."

"Although the UK is divided, the vote will tilt for staying."

Comments like these were being thrown around. My family in the UK who voted to remain were appalled. What now? They worried as their country left the EU and the result was causing such turmoil with the financial markets and immigration—and who knew what more chaos would come from it. My minimal amounts of stocks and bonds to carry me through my retirement were on a teeter-totter because of this.

"Should I stay, or should I sell?"

This upcoming presidential election lay heavily with me. You see, I felt frightened over the possibility that this Brexit vote predicted a Trump victory and that my nation would be in jeopardy as well as the world.

"Should I stay, or should I go?"

I could have gone. I have an EU passport and dual citizenship with Ireland as well as the US. The idea of leaving gave me insight into the dread of having to flee one's country. I was born at the end of

WWII—not that long ago, really. At that time there were thousands of refugees trying to find their families and their way home. Numerous survivors did not want to return to the land they fled from.

All of them were changed significantly by the experience.

"Should I stay, or should I go?"

If I went, things would have to be so unacceptable. I wanted to stay.

WOMEN'S MARCH

I t was January 21, just after the inauguration of the forty-fifth president that I found myself, along with my niece Elizabeth and friends Robert and Nancy, walking down 4th Street to the Metro station on Colorado Ave. It was 7:45 a.m., and throngs of people were heading our way with their pink caps. The Metro was free that day and our ride to the end of the Expo Line was filled to maximum capacity, unable to pick up any more people as it headed into Los Angeles. It took us fifty minutes with no seats, standing room only.

But the energy on this train was jubilant with chanting, singing, and all-around buzzing with excitement.

Once off the train, we followed the flow of human traffic to Pershing Square and were literally pinned there as the streets were completely impacted. We were there an hour and a half before we started moving at a snail's pace toward city hall. We were at least two blocks away and there was another stand-still. The mood was electric with every kind of sign imaginable: "Girls just want to have <u>Fun</u>damental rights!" and a picture of Princess Leia with "Join the resistance" were just a couple of my favorites.

There was such camaraderie amongst strangers and a courteous joyfulness even though we were all uncomfortably squished together. Many would join arms and hands as we moved through the crowds like molasses.

What was stimulating to me was being with so many like-minded people and feeling for the first time in many weeks that hope might be obtainable.

The news that evening was exhilarating with the response that cities around the country and world had showed up in unbelievable numbers. My daughter, Wendy and two granddaughters, Audrey and Katherine, also participated in the Women's March in Boise, Idaho, as did friends of mine in Albuquerque and Santa Fe. They all marched in the snow and rain. Events with kindred spirits in San Francisco, Oakland, and San Luis Obispo had enjoyed massive turnouts. In Los Angeles, 750,000 people attended. Many friends in my hometown marched, but I never saw a one as I scoured the crowds for them.

It was so uncomfortable but I was absolutely

invigorated. How could that be? While physically exhausted, I was mentally refreshed. This was such a juxtaposition.

The fatigue I felt once home was frightening. Larry and I had plans to meet another couple for dinner and it was all I could do to be sociable. I felt old . . . very, very old. Maybe, just maybe, the struggle going on within me due to the negative feelings I'd had about our future and why I had to be part of this march were wearing me down. Never in my lifetime had I possessed such fear.

Do I bury my head in the sand?

Do I get well informed and even madder?

How do we survive in this great America having a "wild card" in charge?

Joining Move-On and another organization in Oregon led to weekly homework such as daily phone calls and postcard writing. This provided me with a sense of belonging to the ranks that were waging battle against this administration. I imagined there were more marches in my future as I would continue fighting for our rights as women as well as those others in our country.

LIFE BEHIND THE MASK

A mask was significant for me as a seventy-four-year-old woman for two reasons: One, it protected me from COVID-19; two, it covered my wrinkly skin and sagging jowls. Ah . . . the event of the coronavirus was a fine time for the older generation! Yes, it was a dangerous time for folks our age; however, if we followed the required guidelines, we had a better chance of avoiding this dreaded virus.

Not being able to travel and go out socially was not such a difficult exercise for me at my age. Traveling was becoming a necessary evil to me. Rushing to the airport in Los Angeles traffic, and then being jostled with the effort of going through security and being cramped in a plane for a few hours at a time was uncomfortable, but it served a means to an end: to see my children in Idaho and my casita in New Mexico. Being forced to remain at home was not a great sacrifice after a while.

BUT—and yes, it was a big BUT—what if I had been in my late teens, twenties, or thirties and young and vibrant and wanting to meet a partner!

Wouldn't I want to wear the latest lipstick and show off my alluring face, smooth and plump??!! How do you do that with a mask? What about parties and clubbing and concerts . . . how do you get a chance to dance and meet others?

Going to college, a once exciting adventure, was being disrupted.

Imagine being unable to attend classes and do all that goes with that experience, like sporting events, dances, and meeting someone you were attracted to but afraid to kiss.

Wearing a mask hid me and was a reminder that you couldn't get too close.

Having a grandchild ready to leave home and attend college and just desiring to do the things young people want to do at that age was reminding me that longing and friskiness were part of youth. That feeling of being immortal would make wearing a mask rather unimportant. What a dilemma!

Wearing a mask at this time was a way of pro-tecting everyone—not just myself but all others. It was the right thing to do. However, I did forgive the youth of the nation. So now it was up to me to stay safe—and wearing my mask did this.

BEHIND THE MASK

A funny thing happened the other day. After looking at myself in the mirror and feeling rather drab, I put on some lipstick to perk me up and give my face a bit of color as I was going to the market. Then on went the mask and my lips were hidden, and my mask needed washing to get the lipstick out! Oh, well . . . I suppose at any age we don't want to be covered up.

GOODBYE, MY FRIEND

As I stood there at Santa Monica Beach thinking of my friend, I could remember us sitting at the water's edge the summer of 1963, letting the residue of foamy white waves wash over our feet, toes dug into the wet sand, lost in family storytelling related to our Irish heritage. His father and my mother were both born and raised in the "old country" and this affected both our young lives in America. Such hopes we had for our futures.

My friend Terry passed away last month. He was writing his memoirs and creating a book of short stories. Terry sent the drafts to me for critiquing. The writing was beautiful! What would happen with it now?

We were high school friends and looked young for our age—more like thirteen than sixteen. Terry would help me with my Latin homework, and we would share our feelings of not fitting into the St. Monica High School culture; we looked too young to be cool.

Our class hung out at Sorrento's—the portion of beach nicknamed after the hamburger stand. This was off the parking lot at the end of the California ramp onto PCH, which was called Sorrento's Grill. Many of our male classmates spent the summer working there, often doling out burgers and fries to us for free.

Terry truly saw me, the frightened little girl always worrying about fitting in, and he seemed to grasp that and support me. He understood living with the conflicting views we both faced growing up with parents from another country who were imposing their traditions onto us—many of which did not coincide with American culture. How freeing it was to have his male point of view and be accepted. More than any other individual in my life at the time, he knew me; an indelible, rich friendship ensued.

After graduating from college with a degree in Spanish, Terry was soon drafted. It was 1968, and he became a helicopter pilot, while I was experiencing the joys of being a new mother, offsetting the obvious turbulence of the late sixties with the assassinations of MLK and Bobby Kennedy and the escalation of war in Southeast Asia.

Terry's service in Vietnam ripped away his joy, laughter, and innocence as surely as the Vietcong wrenched the lives of the young soldiers he had been sent to rescue—men trapped in the jungle under enemy fire, including his best friend. Terry accompanied his friend's body home to Los Angeles and to the wife and new baby girl who awaited the remains.

Terry became an ex-pat living in Europe and Asia, only coming to the States to visit his mother and brothers. I, meanwhile, was writing letters as "Another Mother for Peace" in protest of the war while raising my little girl. Each time he was in town, which was rare, he would call me, and we would get together for a beer. He would never share what happened to him in Vietnam, saying, "The experience is too painful to discuss."

It was only later, through his writing, that I was to find out the horror of those war years.

Some of the things he did share with me were that, after his tour of duty was over, he flew to Spain to live and drown his agony with drink and drugs; he was so disillusioned with the United States, and the ugliness and futility of that war that would not leave his mind. Years passed before he met Hwei, a Taiwanese woman, who helped him get back on his feet.

He taught English and she taught Chinese at the Spanish University; their love for each other grew and eventually they married and had two children together. They were traveling professors spending time in various countries: Scotland, France, and China, just to name a few that I knew about. It was this family that brought him joy.

Our fifty-year high school reunion was in 2013. It had been ages since we had been together, and it was to be the last time I was able to hug my friend. He walked into our venue at the Jonathan Club on the beach right next door to what had been Sorrento's beach. I knew him instantly. His golden curls, around his angelic face, were now salt and pepper, and that sweet, once young face was lined slightly with a short white beard. His eyes were still a haunted dark blue. He was a runner and had a slim body—not tall, about five feet, eight inches. He was still as slight as he had been in high school and looked young for his age, which at sixty-eight was now a good thing. His children were grown and now living in the States. So, he and Hwei had rented an apartment in Brooklyn to be closer to the kids while living most of the year in their cottage in New Zealand.

That evening, we discussed our love of writing. Now that we were both retired, we had the time to pursue it. From then on, we exchanged our writing, and he sent me drafts of his stories. That is when I finally discovered the terror he'd gone through in Vietnam. I shared stories of my father, who had also experienced war, as well as stories of my mother in Ireland.

My friend is gone now after his battle with brain tumors. No more will he suffer as he did that last month as Hwei shared his battle to live, to finish his story, to enjoy his grandchildren.

Goodbye, my friend! You will always live joyfully in my memory!

WRAPPING UP

I am now in the September of my years and am wanting to share some of my life. Because of knowing so little regarding my grandparents, and wishing I had, I decided to write about my life for my remaining family. These short memoir stories are from different periods in my life. Most of these short memories take place where I grew up and lived in Venice and Santa Monica, California. Although I was born in Winnipeg, Canada, my family immigrated to the US when I was two due to the vicious cold of the winters there.

So, I remember my life in California. My parents are now dead and when questions come up, I have no one to ask. My mother spoke of her life, but my father never spoke of his youth except about how much he enjoyed ice skating on the streets of Winnipeg, where he played hockey with his neighbor friends.

Being retired has been a time to write and pursue

the things I could not do while working. I took writing classes to improve my telling of tales to my granddaughters, which I have turned into books about their years from birth to age eighteen. I wanted to capture their lives in an interesting way. I've incorporated stories of my parents, my daughter, and my own life into these stories, as I had no knowledge of my own ancestry.

The pandemic is over, and I am now in Abiquiu, New Mexico, in our lovely casita, which we bought in October 2009, and get to enjoy each year. We have made such treasured friends. There is a significant sadness in me this visit, as a cherished neighbor is dying, and while it is a blessing to be here with him and his family and be able to help, it is painful as he will not be here when we come back in July.

Losing friends is happening more frequently now. Will I ever get used to it? On the positive side, I have many nephews and nieces getting married and having little ones. This is exciting as life goes on regardless. My granddaughters are in college. I learn from them, and we are close, and I'm thrilled to be in their presence. When we are away, we try to see them regularly. My daughter has been the most amazing joy of my life. I am incredibly blessed. Larry and I continue to love each other and laugh lots. We are healthy so far and can walk and travel and take care of ourselves. We have another story coming up—a trip to France, Spain, and Portugal in September. Something more to write about.

Printed in the USA
CPSIA information can be obtained
at www.ICGtesting.com
CBHW071054310724
12436CB00024B/223/J

9 781039 181137